GCSE
Spanish
VOCABULARY BOOK

Terry Murray

EDUCATIONAL

Every effort has been made to trace copyright holders and to obtain their permission for the use of copyright material. The authors and publishers will gladly receive information enabling them to rectify any errors or omission in subsequent editions.

First published 1997
Reprinted 1998

Letts Educational
Schools and Colleges Division
9–15 Aldine Street
London W12 8AW
0181 740 2270

Text: © T.P. Murray 1997
Design and illustrations © BPP (Letts Educational) Ltd 1997

Design and production by Moondisks Ltd, Cambridge

British Library Cataloguing-in-Publication Data
A CIP record for this book is available from the British Library

ISBN 1 84085 1430

Printed and bound in Great Britain

Letts Educational is the trading name of BPP (Letts Educational) Ltd

Acknowledgement
The Useful IT Vocabulary on pages 84–86 is taken from *Modern Languages, Information File No. 16* published in 1991 by the National Council for Educational Technology (NCET) and is reproduced here with the permission of the publishers.

To Michael Henry

Introduction

- This vocabulary book contains the words you need to know for GCSE.
- It has been prepared by a Chief Examiner with a major Exam Board.
- In their GCSE syllabuses all the Exam Boards have a list of about 1500 words: this list is called the Minimum Core Vocabulary.
- The exams are based on these lists.
- There are lots of differences between the lists of different Boards.
- This book tells you which word is listed by which Board.
- The first section of words, Days, Months, etc., is a section common to all Boards.
- Each Exam Board will use words outside its list for the more difficult questions – so you should try to learn all the words in this book.
- All the Exam Boards have the same topic areas: these areas are called the Areas of Experience.
- The words in this book have been categorised into the Areas of Experience which are the topic categories that all Boards use.
- There is also a section on IT vocabulary. These words are not on the Exam Boards' lists.

What you should do

1 Find out from your teacher which Exam Board you will be using.
2 Highlight and learn the words specified by your Board.
3 Concentrate on the Area of Experience that you are working on at school.
4 Remember that you will need to know more words than your Board's Minimum Core Vocabulary.

Learn the words set down by the other Boards.
5 The more dots beside a word, the more that word is important. Learn the important words first.

T.P.M.

Contents

Important words

Useful words

Area of Experience A

Everyday activities

Contents

Area of Experience B

Personal and social life

Area of Experience C

The world around us

Contents

Area of Experience D

The world of work

Area of Experience E

The international world

Important words

Days

los días de la semana	the days of the week
lunes	Monday
martes	Tuesday
miércoles	Wednesday
jueves	Thursday
viernes	Friday
sábado	Saturday
domingo	Sunday

Months

los meses del año	the months of the year
enero	January
febrero	February
marzo	March
abril	April
mayo	May
junio	June
julio	July
agosto	August
setiembre	September
octubre	October
noviembre	November
diciembre	December

Numbers

los números cardinales	cardinal numbers
cero	0
uno	1
dos	2
tres	3
cuatro	4
cinco	5
seis	6
siete	7
ocho	8

nueve	9
diez	10
once	11
doce	12
trece	13
catorce	14
quince	15
dieciséis	16
diecisiete	17
dieciocho	18
diecinueve	19
veinte	20
veintiuno	21
veintidós	22
veintitrés	23
veinticuatro	24
veinticinco	25
veintiséis	26
veintisiete	27
veintiocho	28
veintinueve	29
treinta	30
treinta y uno	31
treinta y dos	32
cuarenta	40
cincuenta	50
sesenta	60
setenta	70
ochenta	80
noventa	90
cien	100
ciento uno	101
ciento noventa	190
doscientos	200
doscientos once	211
mil	1000
dos mil	2000
un millón	1 000 000
dos millones	2 000 000
los números ordinales	ordinal numbers
primero	first
segundo	second
tercero	third
cuarto	fourth

quinto	fifth
sexto	sixth
séptimo	seventh
octavo	eighth
noveno	ninth
décimo	tenth

Time

la hora	the time
¿Qué hora es?	What's the time?
Son las siete	It's seven o'clock
Son las dos y cinco	It's five past two
Son las nueve y cuarto	It's a quarter past nine
Son las cuatro y media	It's half past four
Son las seis menos veinte	It's twenty to six
Es la una menos cuarto	It's a quarter to one
Son las doce	It's twelve o'clock noon/midnight
Son las doce y media	It's half past twelve
A las cuatro y veinticinco de la tarde	At 16.25
A las tres menos cuarto de la tarde	At 14.45
A las seis de la tarde	At 18.00
de la mañana	a.m.
de la tarde	p.m. until dark
de la noche	p.m. after dark
A las cuatro de la mañana	At 4 o'clock in the morning

Date

¿Cuál es la fecha?	What's the date today?
Hoy es lunes trece de enero de mil novecientos noventa y seis	It's Monday the thirteenth of January 1996
El domingo primero de mayo	Sunday the first of May

Seasons

las estaciones del año	the seasons
la primavera	spring
el verano	summer
el otoño	autumn
el invierno	winter
en primavera	in spring
en verano, en otoño, en invierno	in summer/autumn/winter
durante el verano	during the summer

Question words

los interrogativos	question words
¿a qué hora?	what time?
¿de quién? ¿de quiénes?	whose?
¿con quién? ¿con quiénes?	with whom?
¿cuántas veces?	how often?
¿cuánto tiempo?	how long?
¿cuántos? ¿cuántas?	how many?
¿cómo?	how?
¿dónde?	where?
¿por qué?	why?
¿qué?	what?
¿cuándo?	when?
¿quién? ¿quiénes?	who?

Useful words

Quantities

la cantidad	quantity
el centímetro	centimetre
la cucharada	spoonful
la decena de	about ten
la docena	dozen
el gramo	gramme
el kilo	kilo
el kilogramo	kilogramme
el kilómetro	kilometre
el litro	litre
media docena	half dozen
medio kilo	half a kilo
la milla	mile
la mitad	half
el montón	pile
el par	pair
el pedazo	piece
la pieza	piece
por ciento	per cent
el resto	remains
el trozo	piece

Negatives

no ... jamás	never
no ... nada	nothing
no ... nadie	nobody
no ... ni ... ni	neither ... nor
no ... ninguno	no
no ... nunca	never
no ... tampoco	neither

Prepositions

a lo largo de	along
a mediados de	half way through
acerca de	concerning
además de	in addition to
alrededor de	around
bajo	under
a causa de	because of
cerca de	near
con	with
contra	against
debajo de	under
delante de	in front of
desde	since
después de	after
detrás de	behind
durante	during
en medio de	in the middle of
encima de	above
enfrente de	opposite
entre	between, among
al final de	at the end of
fuera de	outside
hacia	towards
hasta	until
junto a	next to
al lado de	beside
lejos de	far from
a orillas de	on the banks of
para	for
por	for, through, by
según	according to
sin	without
sobre	on
tras	behind
a través de	across

'Tener' expressions

tener calor	to be hot
tener dieciséis años	to be sixteen
tener dolor de …	to have a sore …
tener éxito	to be successful
tener fiebre	to have a temperature
tener frío	to be cold
tener ganas de	to want to
tener hambre	to be hungry
tener lugar	to take place
tener miedo	to be frightened
tener prisa	to be in a hurry
tener que	to have to
tener razón	to be right
tener sed	to be thirsty
tener sueño	to be sleepy
tener suerte	to be lucky

Other words and expressions

a propósito	by the way
algo	something
alguien	somebody
alguno	some
aquel	that
así	so
aun	even
aunque	although
como	as
con respecto a	regarding
conmigo, contigo	with me, with you
al contrario	on the contrary
entretanto	meanwhile
incluso	even
mientras	while
pero	but
por lo tanto	therefore
porque	because
pues	then
puesto que	since
quizá(s)	perhaps

si	if
sin embargo	however
sobre todo	especially
tal	such
tal vez	perhaps
tan	so
unos	some
ya que	since

Everyday activities

Home life

At home

el aire climatizado	air conditioning
el aire acondicionado	air conditioning
el balcón	balcony
la barrera	fence
la bombilla	light-bulb
la calefacción central	central heating
la casa	house
la cerradura	lock
la chimenea	fireplace/chimney
la cortina	curtain
el cristal	pane of glass
el cuadro	picture
el cubo de la basura	rubbish bin
la electricidad	electricity
el electrodoméstico	electrical appliances
el interruptor	switch
la lámpara	lamp
la luz	light
el magnetofón	tape recorder
los muebles	furniture
el objeto	object
la papelera	waste-paper basket
la pared	wall
la persiana	blinds
la pintura	painting
el primer piso	first floor
la puerta	door
la puerta principal	front door
el radiador	radiator
el reloj	clock
el rincón	corner (inside)
el suelo	floor
la tabla	plank, board

MEG NEAB ULEAC SEG WJEC NICCEA

el techo — ceiling
el tejado — roof
la ventana — window

The rooms

el comedor — dining room
el cuarto de baño — bathroom
el cuarto de estar — lounge
la cueva — wine cellar
el desván — attic
el dormitorio — bedroom
la entrada — entrance
la escalera — stairs
el estudio — study
el garaje — garage
la habitación — room
el hogar — home
el pasillo — corridor
el patio — patio, yard
el piso — floor
la planta baja — ground floor
la sala de estar — lounge
el salón — lounge
el sótano — basement
el vestíbulo — hall

Materials

el acero — steel
el algodón — cotton
el cuero — leather
el hierro — iron
la lana — wool
la madera — wood
el mármol — marble
el nilón — nylon
el oro — gold
la piel — leather
la plata — silver
el plomo — lead

la seda — silk
el vidrio — glass

Adjectives

amueblado — furnished
anterior — previous
cómodo — comfortable
completo — full
final — final
ideal — ideal
igual — same
importante — important
incómodo — uncomfortable
interior — interior
lujoso — luxurious
magnífico — magnificent
mismo — same
moderno — modern
otro — another
preciso — necessary
privado — private
viejo — old

Verbs

afeitarse — to shave
apagar — to switch off (e.g. light)
aparcar — to park
arrancar — to start
barrer — to sweep
calentar — to heat
casarse — to get married
cepillarse — to brush (i.e. teeth)
cerrar — to close
cerrar con llave — to lock
cocinar — to cook
coger — to get
colgar — to hang
colocar — to place
compartir — to share

	MEG	MEG	NEAB	ULEAC	SEG	WJEC	NICCEA

congelar — to freeze

dejar — to let, to leave

descansar — to rest

desnudarse — to get undressed

despertarse — to wake up

dormir — to sleep

dormirse — to fall asleep

ducharse — to have a shower

encender la luz — to switch on the light

encontrar — to meet, to find

encontrarse — to be found

estar — to be

fregar — to scrub

freír — to fry

funcionar — to work (of machinery)

lavar — to wash

lavar los platos — to wash the dishes

lavarse — to get washed

lavarse la cabeza — to wash one's hair

lavarse los dientes — to clean one's teeth

levantarse — to get up

limpiar — to clean

madrugar — to get up early

manchar — to stain

morder — to bite

pasar la aspiradora — to do the vacuuming

peinarse — to comb one's hair

planchar — to iron

poder — to be able

poner la mesa — to lay the table

quitar la mesa — to clear the table

quitarse la ropa — to take off clothes

rasgar — to tear

renovar — to renew

reparar — to repair

sacar — to take out, to buy (a ticket)

secar — to dry

soñar — to dream

utilizar — to use

vaciar	to empty
vestirse	to get dressed

The living room

la alfombra	carpet
la butaca	armchair
el canapé	settee
la cómoda	chest of drawers
la estantería	shelves
la moqueta	carpet
el sillón	armchair
el sofá	settee

The bedroom

la agenda	diary
la almohada	pillow
el cajón	drawer
la cama	bed
la cama de matrimonio	double bed
el colchón	mattress
el despertador	alarm clock
el estante	shelf
el guardarropa	wardrobe
la manta	blanket
el póster	poster
la sábana	sheet
el secador	hairdryer
el tocador	dressing table

The bathroom

el baño	bath
el cepillo de dientes	toothbrush
el champú	shampoo
la ducha	shower
el espejo	mirror
el jabón	soap
el lavabo	washbasin
el maquillaje	make-up
la máquina de afeitar	electric shaver

el papel higiénico	toilet paper
la pasta de dientes	toothpaste
el peine	comb
el perfume	perfume
el taburete	stool
las tijeras	scissors
la toalla	towel

The kitchen

el abrelatas	tin-opener
el aparador	sideboard
el armario	cupboard
la bandeja	tray
la cacerola	saucepan
la cocina	kitchen
la cocina	cooker
la cocina de gas	gas cooker
la cocina eléctrica	electric cooker
el congelador	freezer
el fregadero	sink
el frigorífico	fridge
el grifo	tap
el horno	oven
la jarra	jug
la lata	tin
la lavadora	washing machine
el lavaplatos	dishwasher
la mesa	table
la nevera	fridge
el olor	smell
el sacacorchos	corkscrew
la sartén	frying pan
la silla	chair
la taza	cup
el tisú	tissue
la vajilla	crockery

MEG MEG MEG MEG MEG NEAB ULEAC SEG SEG WJEC WJEC NICCEA

The garden

el árbol	tree
el arbusto	shrub
el césped	lawn
la flor	flower
la hierba	grass
el jardín	garden
el manzano	apple tree
el muro	wall
la planta	plant
la rama	branch
la rosa	rose
el sendero	path
la violeta	violet

Pets

la cobaya	hamster
el conejo	rabbit
el gato	cat
el hámster	hamster
el insecto palo	stick insect
la jaula	cage
los peces tropicales	tropical fish
el periquito	parakeet
el perro	dog
el pez	fish
el ratón	mouse
la tortuga	tortoise

The housework

la aguja	needle
el agujero	hole
el alfiler	pin
la aspiradora	vacuum cleaner
la basura	rubbish
el cepillo	brush
la faena de casa	chore
el hilo	thread
la mancha	stain

el orden	order (i.e. tidiness)
la plancha	iron
el polvo	dust
los quehaceres	chores

Houses

la casa adosada	semi-detached house
la casa de campo	country house
la casa de un piso	bungalow
la casa independiente	detached house

School

In class

el acento	accent
los apuntes	notes
la asignatura	subject
la atención	attention
el aula (f)	classroom
el bachillerato	A-level
la cartelera	notice board
la casilla	box (on exam paper)
el castigo	punishment
la clase	class
el colegio	school
el conocimiento	knowledge
la contestación	answer
los corregidos	corrections
el COU	pre-university year
el curso	course
los deberes	homework
el detalle	detail
el dibujo	drawing
el diccionario	dictionary
la disciplina	discipline
la educación	education
el ejemplo	example
el ejercicio	exercise

Spanish	English	MEG	NEAB	ULEAC	SEG	WJEC	NICCEA
el error	mistake						
el esfuerzo	effort						
los estudios	studies						
el examen	exam						
la excepción	exception						
la figura	shape						
la frase	sentence						
el gimnasio	gymnasium						
la gramática	grammar						
hacer preguntas	to ask questions						
el informe	piece of information						
el intercambio	school exchange						
el/la interno/a	boarder						
la lección	lesson						
la letra	letter (e.g. of alphabet)						
el método	method						
el modo	way, manner						
la nota	mark						
el número	number						
la orden	command						
la página	page						
la palabra	word						
el papel	paper						
el pasado	past						
el permiso	permission						
la pizarra	blackboard						
la pregunta	question						
el progreso	progress						
la prueba	test						
el pupitre	desk						
el recreo	break						
la respuesta	answer						
la sección	section						
la tarea	homework						
el timbre	bell						
la tiza	chalk						
el trimestre	term						
el uniforme	uniform						
el vocabulario	vocabulary						
la vuelta al colegio	return to school						

Subjects

el arte	art
la biología	biology
el castellano	Spanish language
las ciencias	sciences
el drama	drama
la economía	economics
la educación física	PE
la física	physics
la geografía	geography
la gimnasia	gym
la historia	history
los idiomas	languages
la informática	IT
la literatura	literature
las matemáticas	maths
la mecanografía	typing
la música	music
la química	chemistry
la tecnología	technology
los trabajos manuales	CDT

Adjectives

aburrido	bored
afortunado	fortunate
antiguo	old, former
ausente	absent
autorizado	permitted
calificado	qualified
católico	Catholic
correcto	correct
cristiano	Christian
estricto	strict
exigente	demanding
fácil	easy
festivo (día festivo)	holiday
incorrecto	incorrect
injusto	injust
lógico	logic
mixto	mixed

necesario	necessary
obligatorio	compulsory
parecido	similar
particular	private
pobre	poor
posible	possible
presente	present
probable	probable
propio	own
público	public
querido	dear (in a letter)
retrasado	delayed
severo	severe
sorprendente	surprising

The places

la cantina	dining area
el colegio mixto	mixed school
el colegio técnico	technical school
la escuela	primary school
el instituto	school
el laboratorio	lab

The equipment

el aparato	piece of equipment
el boli	pen
el bolígrafo	pen
la calculadora	calculator
la cosa	thing
el cuaderno	exercise book
la fotocopiadora	photocopier
la goma	rubber
la hoja de papel	sheet of paper
el lápiz	pencil
el libro	book
el libro de texto	text book
el ordenador	computer
la regla	ruler

el rotulador — felt-tip pen
el sacapuntas — pencil sharpener

The people

el/la alumno/a — pupil
el conserje — caretaker
el/la director/a — headteacher
el/la estudiante — student
el/la idiota — idiot
el/la imbécil — imbecile
el profesor — teacher
el tutor — tutor

Verbs

aburrirse — to be bored
acabar de — to have just
aguantar — to put up with
añadir — to add
aprender — to learn
aprobar — to pass (an exam)
arreglar — to sort out
calcular — to calculate
castigar — to punish
comenzar — to begin
comparar — to compare
comprender — to understand
continuar — to continue
copiar — to copy
corregir — to correct
deber — to have to
dejar el colegio — to leave school
deletrear — to spell
devolver — to give back
dibujar — to draw
doblar — to double
educar — to educate, to bring up
empezar — to begin
empujar — to push
enseñar — to teach

MEG NEAB ULEAC SEG WJEC NICCEA

entender	to understand
escoger	to choose
escuchar	to listen
estudiar	to study
examinarse	to take an exam
explicar	to explain
fracasar	to fail
inquietarse	to worry
interesarse por	to be interested in
levantar la mano	to raise one's hand
lograr	to succeed
necesitar	to need
ofrecer	to offer
olvidarse de	to forget
organizar	to organise
pasar lista	to call the register
pelear	to fight
permitir	to allow
poner	to put
ponerse a	to begin to
preguntar	to ask
preocuparse	to worry
preparar	to prepare
prohibir	to forbid
querer decir	to mean
repasar	to revise
repetir	to repeat
responder	to answer
resultar	to turn out
revisar	to check
sacar buenas notas	to get good marks
sacar malas notas	to get bad marks
significar	to mean
sonar	to sound
subrayar	to underline
suspender	to fail (exam)
sustituir	to substitute
terminar	to finish
traducir	to translate
valer	to be worth

Food and drink

Meals

el almuerzo	lunch
la cena	evening meal
el desayuno	breakfast
la merienda	snack/picnic

Vegetables

el ajo	garlic
la cebolla	onion
el champiñon	mushroom
la col	cabbage
las coles de Bruselas	sprouts
la coliflor	cauliflower
el espárrago	asparagus
las espinacas	spinach
el guisante	pea
el haba (f)	bean
las judías verdes	green beans
la lechuga	lettuce
las legumbres	vegetables
la patata	potato
el pepino	cucumber
el pimiento	pepper
las verduras	vegetables
la zanahoria	carrot

Fruit

el albaricoque	apricot
la almendra	almond
la cereza	cherry
la ciruela	plum
la frambuesa	raspberry
la fresa	strawberry
la fruta	fruit
el higo	fig

el limón	lemon
la manzana	apple
el melocotón	peach
el melón	melon
la naranja	orange
la pera	pear
la piña	pineapple
el plátano	banana
la sandía	water melon
el tomate	tomato
la uva	grape

Meat

el biftec	steak
el bistec	steak
la carne	meat
la carne de cerdo	pork
la carne de cordero	lamb
la carne de ternera	veal
la carne de vaca	beef
el chorizo	garlic sausage
la chuleta	chop
el cordero	lamb
el filete	fillet
el jamón	ham
el jamón de York	York ham
el jamón serrano	cured ham
el pollo	chicken
el salchichón	garlic sausage
el solomillo	sirloin
la ternera	veal
el tocino	bacon

On the table

el aceite	oil
el azúcar	sugar
los cubiertos	cutlery
la cuchara	spoon
el cuchillo	knife

23

				MEG	NEAB	ULEAC	SEG	WJEC	NICCEA

el mantel — tablecloth
la pimienta — pepper
el platillo — saucer
el plato — dish
el porrón — wine jar
la sal — salt
la salsa — sauce
la servilleta — serviette
el tenedor — fork
el vinagre — vinegar

Other food

el aceite de oliva — olive oil
la aceituna — olive
el arroz — rice
la barra — loaf
el bizcocho — sponge cake
el bocadillo — sandwich (French bread)
los bombones — chocolates
el caramelo — sweet
el chocolate — chocolate
el churro — fritter
el cocido — stew
la ensalada — salad
la ensaladilla — Russian salad
la galleta — biscuit
la hamburguesa — hamburger
la harina — flour
el helado — ice-cream
el huevo — egg
la mayonesa — mayonnaise
el panecillo — roll
las patatas fritas — chips
el perrito caliente — hot dog
la salchicha — sausage
el sandwich — sandwich
el termo — thermos flask
la tortilla — omelette
la tortilla española — Spanish omelette
el yogur — yogurt

Starters

el aperitivo	appetiser
los entremeses	starters
el gazpacho	cold soup
la sopa	soup

From the sea/river

el atún	tunny fish
el bacalao	cod
los calamares	squid
el cangrejo	crab
las gambas	prawns
la langosta	crab
el lenguado	sole
los mariscos	seafood
los mejillones	mussels
la merluza	hake
el pescado	fish
la sardina	sardine
la trucha	trout

Desserts

el flan	caramel custard
la nata	cream
el pastel	cake
el postre	dessert
el pudín	(bread) pudding
el queso	cheese
la tarta	cake, tart, pie
la torta	cake
el turrón	nougat

Breakfast

los cereales	cereals
la mantequilla	butter
la mermelada	jam
el pan	bread
el pan tostado	toasted bread
la tostada	toast

Drinks

el agua (m)	water
el agua mineral con gas	mineral water (fizzy)
el agua mineral sin gas	mineral water (still)
la bebida	drink
la cerveza	beer
el champán	champagne
la coca-cola	coca-cola
el coñac	coñac
la gaseosa	lemonade
la ginebra	gin
el gin tonic	gin and tonic
la horchata	almond drink
el jerez	sherry
el jugo de fruta	fruit juice
la leche	milk
la limonada	lemonade
la manzanilla	manzanilla sherry
la naranjada	orange squash
el refresco	soft drink
la sangría	sangria
la sidra	cider
el té	tea
el tinto	red wine
el vino	wine
el zumo de fruta	fruit juice
el zumo de naranja	orange juice

The restaurant

los aseos	toilets
la bandeja	tray
la botella	bottle
el/la camarero/a	waiter/waitress
la comida	food
los cubiertos	cutlery
la especialidad	speciality
el menú del día	set menu of the day
el plato combinado	set meal
por aquí	this way
el precio fijo	fixed price

la receta	recipe
el restaurante	restaurant
el sabor	flavour
el servicio	service
los servicios	toilets
el/la vegetariano/a	vegetarian

The café

la bandeja	tray
el café	coffee
el café con leche	white coffee
el café solo	black coffee
la cafetería	café
el cenicero	ashtray
cobrar	to charge
la copa	glass
la cuenta	bill
el hielo	ice
el mostrador	counter
nada más	that's all
la propina	tip
la ración	portion
la ronda	round (of drinks)
la sombra	shade
las tapas	bar snacks
la tarifa	price list
la terraza	terrace
el trapo	rag, cloth
el vaso	glass
el vino blanco	white wine
el vino tinto	red wine

Adjectives

asado	roast
barato	cheap
caro	expensive
congelado	frozen
costoso	dear
delicioso	delicious

dulce	sweet
frito	fried
gratis	free
gratuito	free
incluido	included
inevitable	inevitable
libre	free
picante	hot (to the taste)
potable	drinkable
próximo	next
variado	varied

Restaurant verbs

almorzar	to have lunch
aprovecharse	to take advantage of
bastar	to be enough
beber	to drink
cenar	to have dinner
comer	to eat
desayunar	to have breakfast
helar	to freeze
hervir	to boil
merendar	to have a snack/picnic
oler a	to smell of
pagar	to pay
pedir	to ask for, to order
probar	to try out
quejarse	to complain
quitar	to remove
saber a	to taste of
servir	to serve
traer	to bring
tragar	to swallow

Health and fitness

	MEG	NEAB	ULEAC	SEG	WJEC	NICCEA

Sports

el alpinismo	climbing, mountaineering
el atletismo	athletics
el baloncesto	basketball
el balonvolea	volleyball
el billar	billiards
el ciclismo	cycling
la corrida de toros	bullfight
la equitación	horse-riding
el esquí acuático	water ski-ing
el fútbol	football
el futbolín	table football
la natación	swimming
el patinaje	skating
la pesca	fishing
el ping-pong	table tennis
el tenis	tennis
el windsurf	windsurfing

Sport words

la actividad	activity
el balón	ball
la bicicleta	bicycle
el campeonato	championship
la caña de pescar	fishing rod
la carrera	race
el centro polideportivo	sports centre
la competición	competition
el concurso	competition
la copa mundial	World Cup
la decisión	decision
el deporte	sport
el esquí	ski
el estadio	stadium
la etapa	stage
el fracaso	failure

el gol	goal
las instrucciones	instructions
el juego	game
la liga	league
el partido	match
el paso	step
la pelota	ball
el peso	weight
el premio	prize
el punto	point
la red	net
el resultado	result
el salto	jump
la selección	team
la temporada	season
el terreno	pitch
el torneo	tournament
la vela	sail
el vestuario	dressing room

The people

el/la aficionado/a	fan
el árbitro	referee
el/la atleta	athlete
el/la campeón/campeona	champion
el/la ciclista	cyclist
el equipo	team
el/la espectador/a	spectator
el/la futbolista	footballer
el gamberro	hooligan
el hincha	fan
el/la jugador/a	player
el matador	bullfighter
el miembro	member
el socio	member
el/la tenista	tennis player
el torero	bullfighter

MEG NEAB ULEAC SEG WJEC NICCEA

Verbs

agotar	to exhaust
arrojar	to throw
asistir a	to be present at
asomarse	to lean out of (e.g. a window)
buscar	to look for, to fetch
caerse	to fall
cansarse	to get tired
celebrarse	to take place
correr	to run
dar	to give
echar	to throw
empatar	to draw (a game)
entrenarse	to go training
esconder	to hide
estrenar	to have its première
ganar	to win
intentar	to try
jugar	to play
lanzar	to throw
marcar un gol	to score a goal
meter	to put
montar a caballo	to ride
nadar	to swim
participar	to take part
perder	to lose
pisar	to tread
practicar	to practise
respirar	to breathe
saltar	to jump
silbar	to whistle
sudar	to sweat
tirar	to pull
torear	to bullfight
vencer	to beat
zambullirse	to dive

The body

la barba	beard
el bigote	moustache

MEG MEG MEG MEG MEG MEG MEG
NEAB NEAB NEAB NEAB NEAB NEAB NEAB
ULEAC ULEAC ULEAC ULEAC ULEAC ULEAC ULEAC
SEG SEG SEG SEG SEG SEG SEG
WJEC WJEC WJEC WJEC WJEC WJEC WJEC
NICCEA NICCEA NICCEA NICCEA NICCEA NICCEA NICCEA

la boca	mouth
el brazo	arm
el cabello	hair
la cabeza	head
la cara	face
la cintura	waist
el codo	elbow
el corazón	heart
el cuello	neck
el cuerpo	body
el dedo	finger
el diente	tooth
la espalda	back
el estómago	stomach
la frente	forehead
la garganta	throat
el hombro	shoulder
el hueso	bone
el labio	lip
la lágrima	tear
la lengua	tongue
la mano	hand
la mejilla	cheek
la muñeca	wrist
el muslo	thigh
la nariz	nose
el ojo	eye
la oreja	ear
el pecho	chest/breast
el pelo	hair
el pie	foot
la piel	skin
la pierna	leg
la rodilla	knee
el rostro	face
el tobillo	ankle
el vientre	stomach
la voz	voice

MEG NEAB ULEAC SEG WJEC NICCEA

Illnesses

la aspirina	aspirin
el catarro	cold
la cita	appointment (e.g. with doctor)
la clínica	clinic
el comprimido	tablet
la consulta	doctor's surgery, examination
el consultorio	doctor's surgery
la crema	cream
la cura	cure
el diente	tooth
el dolor	pain
la droga	drug
el empaste	filling
la enfermedad	illness
la enteritis	enteritis
el esparadrapo	sticking plaster
la farmacia	chemist's
la fiebre	temperature
la gastritis	gastritis
la gripe	flu
la herida	wound
la insolación	sunstroke
la inyección	injection
el jarabe	syrup
el medicamento	medicine
la medicina	medicine
la muela	tooth (molar)
la operación	operation
la pastilla	tablet
la picadura	bite (insect)
la pomada	cream
la quemadura	burn
el remedio	remedy
el resfriado	cold
la salud	health
el sarampión	measles
el SIDA	AIDS
el síntoma	symptom
el supositorio	suppository

la tirita	sticking plaster
la tos	cough
el tratamiento	treatment
la venda	bandage

The people

el dentista	dentist
el doctor	doctor
el/la enfermero/a	nurse
el/la farmacéutico/a	chemist
el/la médico/a	doctor

Verbs

cortar	to cut
descubrir	to discover
desmayarse	to faint
doler	to hurt
empastar	to put in a filling
estar bien	to feel OK
estar constipado	to have a cold
estar mal	to feel ill
guardar cama	to stay in bed
mantener	to maintain
marearse	to get dizzy
matar	to kill
medir	to measure
picar	to bite
quemar	to burn
quemarse	to burn oneself
remediar	to put right
resbalar	to slip
sentirse	to feel
temblar	to shiver
torcer	to turn, to twist
toser	to cough
vendar	to bandage
vivir	to live
vomitar	to vomit

Personal and social life

Self, family and personal relationships

		MEG	NEAB	ULEAC	SEG	WJEC	NICCEA

Family

el apellido	surname
el bebé	baby
el beso	kiss
la dirección	address
el divorcio	divorce
el domicilio	address
la edad	age
el estado civil	status
la fecha de nacimiento	date of birth
el lugar de nacimiento	place of birth
el nacimiento	birth
el noviazgo	engagement

The people (in the family)

el/la abuelo/a	grandfather/mother
el/la cuñado/a	brother/sister-in-law
el/la esposo/a	husband/wife
la familia	family
los familiares	relations
el gemelo	twin
el/la hermano/a	brother/sister
el/la hijo/a	son/daughter
la madre	mother
la mamá	mum
el marido	husband
la mujer	wife
el/la nieto/a	grandson/daughter
el/la niño/a	child
el/la novio/a	boy/girl friend
la nuera	daughter-in-law
el padre	father
los padres	parents

el papá	dad
el/la pariente	relation
el/la primo/a	cousin
el/la sobrino/a	nephew/niece
el/la suegro/a	father/mother-in-law
el/la tío/a	uncle/aunt
el/la viudo/a	widower/widow
el yerno	son-in-law

Friends

el abrazo	embrace
la amistad	friendship
el amor	love
el apodo	nickname
la bienvenida	welcome
la broma	joke
el carácter	character
el cariño	affection
la carta	letter
el chiste	joke
la cita	date (i.e. to meet friend)
la conversación	conversation
la correspondencia	correspondence
la culpa	blame
los demás	the rest
el deseo	desire
el diálogo	conversation
el favor	favour
el gusto	pleasure
el humor	humour
la identidad	identity
la invitación	invitation
el matrimonio	marriage
la pelea	fight
la postal	postcard
la promesa	promise
la señal	sign, signal
la sonrisa	smile
la tarjeta	card
la visita	visit

People

el/la adolescente	adolescent
el/la adulto/a	adult
el/la amigo/a	friend
el caballero	gentleman
el/la chico/a	boy/girl
el/la compañero/a	friend
el/la correspondiente	penfriend
el/la corresponsal	correspondent
el desconocido	stranger
el/la enemigo/a	enemy
la gente	people
el hombre	man
el huésped	guest
el/la invitado/a	guest
el/la muchacho/a	boy/girl
la pareja	couple
la persona	person
todo el mundo	everybody
el/la vecino/a	neighbour

Verbs

acompañar	to accompany
acordarse	to remember
ayudar	to help
besar	to kiss
cartearse	to exchange letters
celebrar	to celebrate
charlar	to chat
citarse	to arrange to meet
conocer	to know
contar	to tell, to count
contar con	to rely on
crecer	to grow
cumplir	to reach (a birthday)
dar de beber	to give a drink
dar de comer	to feed
dar la mano	to shake hands
dar las gracias	to thank
darse cuenta de	to realise

despedirse de	to say goodbye to
detestar	to hate
divorciarse	to get divorced
echar de menos	to miss (i.e. a person)
echar una carta	to post
elegir	to choose
emparejar	to pair up
enamorarse	to fall in love
encantar	to delight
enfadarse	to get angry
evitar	to avoid
importar	to be important
indicar	to indicate
invitar	to invite
llamarse	to be called
llevarse bien con	to get on well with
llevarse mal con	to get on badly with
llorar	to cry
morir	to die
nacer	to be born
odiar	to hate
parecer	to seem
parecerse a	to be like
pedir un favor	to ask a favour
ponerse	to become
preferir	to prefer
presentar	to introduce
prometer	to promise
proponer	to propose
querer	to love, to want
recoger	to pick up
reconocer	to recognise
recordar	to remember
regalar	to give a present
reírse	to laugh
rogar	to ask
salir	to go out
saludar	to greet
sonreírse	to smile
tutear	to use 'tú'

ver	to see
visitar	to visit

Clothes

el abrigo	overcoat
la americana	jacket
el bañador	swimsuit
la bata	dressing gown
la blusa	blouse
el bolsillo	pocket
la bota	boot
el botón	button
los calcetines	socks
el calzado	footwear
la camisa	shirt
la camiseta	t-shirt
el chaleco	waistcoat
el chandal	tracksuit
la chaqueta	jacket
la cinta	ribbon
el cinturón	belt
la corbata	tie
la falda	skirt
la gorra	cap
el guante	glove
el impermeable	raincoat
el jersey	jersey
los leotardos	tights
la mantilla	mantilla
las medias	stockings/tights
el pantalón corto	shorts
el pantalón vaquero	jeans
los pantalones/el pantalón	trousers
el panty/panti	tights
el pañuelo	handkerchief
el pijama	pyjamas
la rebeca	cardigan
la ropa	clothes
la ropa interior	underclothes
la sandalia	sandal

el sombrero	hat
los tejanos	jeans
la tela	cloth
el traje	suit
el traje de baño	swimsuit
los vaqueros	jeans
el vestido	dress
la zapatilla	slipper
el zapato	shoe
los zapatos de deporte	trainers

Extras

el abanico	fan
el anillo	ring
el billetero	wallet
el bolso de mano	handbag
el broche	brooch
la cartera	briefcase/wallet
el collar	necklace
el diamante	diamond
las gafas	glasses
las gafas de sol	sun glasses
la joya	jewel
las lentillas	lenses
el monedero	purse
el paraguas	umbrella
el pendiente	earring
la pulsera	bracelet
el reloj de pulsera	wristwatch
la sortija	ring

Free time and social activities

Free time

el bañador	swimsuit
la cámara	camera
la caña de pescar	fishing rod
la canción	song

MEG NEAB ULEAC SEG WJEC NICCEA

las cartas	playing cards
el cigarrillo	cigarette
el cigarro	cigar
la colección	collection
el/la deportista	sportsperson
la diapositiva	slide (photo)
el disco	record
la discoteca	disco
la diversión	entertainment
el encendedor	cigarette lighter
el espectáculo	show
el fin	end
la foto(grafía)	photo(graph)
la función	function
la gana	desire
el interés	interest
el juego	game
el juguete	toy
la lotería	lottery
la moda	fashion
el ocio	leisure
el pasatiempo	hobby
el payaso	clown
el premio gordo	first prize
el puro	cigar
los ratos libres	free time
la risa	laughter
el sorteo	draw (i.e. lottery)
la sugerencia	suggestion
el tabaco	tobacco
el tiempo libre	free time
el tocadiscos	record player

Places

la bolera	bowling alley
el circo	circus
el club	club
el club para jóvenes	youth club
el concierto	concert
la exposición	exhibition

el parque de atracciones	theme park
la piscina	swimming pool
la pista de hielo	ice rink
la sala	room
la sala de fiestas	dance hall
la taberna	pub
el zoo	zoo

Activities

el ajedrez	chess
el baile	dance
los bolos	bowling
la caza	hunting
la cerámica	pottery
la cocina	cooking
el corte y confección	dressmaking
el crucigrama	crossword
el deporte	sport
el flamenco	flamenco
el footing	jogging
el monopatín	skateboard
el paseo	walk
el videojuego	video game

Verbs (movement)

acercarse a	to approach
acostarse	to go to bed
adelantar	to overtake
alejarse	to go away
andar	to walk
atravesar	to cross
bajar	to go down
darse prisa	to hurry
dirigirse hacia	to head for
ir	to go
ir a buscar	to fetch
ir a ver	to go and see
irse	to go away
marcharse	to go away

moverse	to move
mudarse	to move house
regresar	to return
subir	to go up
venir	to come
volver	to return
volverse	to turn round

Reading

la ciencia-ficción	science fiction
el diario	newspaper
el fascículo	instalment
la lectura	reading
el libro	book
la novela	novel
el periódico	newspaper
la prensa	press
la revista	magazine
el tebeo	comic

Cinema

el cine	cinema
la comedia	comedy
los dibujos animados	cartoon
la estrella del cine	cinema star
el éxito	success
la fila	row
la localidad	seat, ticket
la obra de teatro	play
la película	film
la película de amor	romantic film
la película de aventuras	adventure film
la película de ciencia-ficción	science-fiction film
la película de miedo	horror film
la película del oeste	western
la película policíaca	detective film
la sesión	performance

43

Music

la banda	band
la canción	song
el cassette	cassette
clásico	classical
el compact disc	compact disc
el conjunto	group
el coro	choir
el disco compacto	CD
el estéreo	stereo
el grupo	group
el instrumento	instrument
la música	music
la música clásica	classical music
la música fuerte	loud music
la música pop	pop music
el/la músico/a	musician
la orquesta	orchestra
el teclado	keyboard

Musical instruments

las castañuelas	castanets
la flauta	flute
la guitarra	guitar
el piano	piano
el violín	violin

TV

la actriz	actress
la charla	chat
el documental	documentary
el episodio	episode
las noticias	news
la pantalla	screen
el programa	programme
la publicidad	advertising
la radio	radio
la tele	TV
el telediario	TV news

MEG NEAB ULEAC SEG WJEC NICCEA

la telenovela	soap
la televisión	TV
el televisor	TV set
la TVE	Spanish TV
el vídeo	video

Verbs

abrazar	to embrace
acudir	to come
bailar	to dance
cantar	to sing
cazar	to hunt
cesar de	to stop (doing something)
coleccionar	to collect
conseguir	to manage
coser	to sew
dar un paseo	to go for a walk
dar una vuelta	to go for a walk
divertirse	to enjoy oneself
fabricar	to make
fumar	to smoke
gustar	to please
huir	to flee
ir de paseo	to go for a walk
leer	to read
pasarlo bien	to have a good time
pasearse	to go for a walk
patinar	to skate
pescar	to fish
pintar	to paint
registrar	to record
seguir	to follow, to continue
señalar	to point out
sentarse	to sit down
separarse	to separate
tocar	to touch, to play
tumbarse	to lie down
usar	to use

Holidays

On holiday

el alojamiento	lodgings
el alquiler	rent
la cámara	camera
la crema bronceadora	sun cream
el descanso	rest
la dificultad	difficulty
el disgusto	annoyance, bother
la distracción	entertainment
el documento	document
la estancia	stay
la excursión	trip
los gastos	expenses
la información	information
el mapa	map
la máquina de fotos	camera
la mochila	rucksack
el regalo	present
el regreso	return
la tarjeta postal	postcard
el trayecto	journey
el/la turista	tourist
el/la veraneante	holiday maker

Camping

los aseos	toilets
el camping	campsite
el/la campista	camper
la caravana	caravan
la cerilla	match
el espacio	space
la facilidad	facility
el gas	gas
la pila	battery
el saco de dormir	sleeping bag
la sala de juegos	games room

| el sitio | place, spot |
| la tienda de campaña | tent |

Hotel

el ascensor	lift
los aseos	toilets
la cadena (de hoteles)	chain (of hotels)
con vista a	with a view of
el/la dueño/a	owner
la ficha	form
la firma	signature
fuera de servicio	out of order
la habitación	room
la habitación doble	double room
la habitación individual	single room
la habitación sencilla	single room
la hoja	form
el hotel	hotel
el hotelero	hotel-owner
el libro de reclamaciones	complaints book
la llave	key
el lujo	luxury
la media pensión	half board
la nacionalidad	nationality
el nombre (de pila)	(first) name
el país de origen	country of origin
el parador	government-run hotel
el pasaporte	passport
la pensión	boarding house
la pensión completa	full board
el portero	hotel porter
prohibida la entrada	no entry
el/la propietario/a	owner
la queja	complaint
la recepción	reception
el/la recepcionista	receptionist
el retrete	toilet
la salida	exit
las señas	address

la vista	view
el wáter	toilet

Verbs

abrir	to open
abrir el grifo	to turn on the tap
acampar	to camp
aguardar	to wait for
ahorrar	to save
alegrarse	to be happy
alojarse	to stay (e.g. in a hotel)
alquilar	to hire
asegurar	to insure
aterrizar	to land
atrasar	to delay
averiarse	to break down
bañarse	to bathe
broncearse	to get tanned
campar	to camp
cerrar el grifo	to turn off the tap
coger una insolación	to get sunstroke
completar	to complete
comprobar	to check
comunicar	to communicate
conducir	to drive
desembarcar	to disembark
despegar	to take off (plane)
desviar	to make a detour
detenerse	to stop
durar	to last
embarcarse	to embark
entrar	to enter
escaparse	to escape
esperar	to wait, to hope, to expect
esquiar	to ski
estacionar	to park
estropear	to spoil
firmar	to sign
flotar	to float
frecuentar	to frequent

	MEG	NEAB	ULEAC	SEG	WJEC	NICCEA

frenar	to brake					
hacer camping	to go camping					
hacer las maletas	to pack					
hallar	to find					
hospedarse	to stay					
informarse	to find out					
ir de camping	to go camping					
ir de vacaciones	to go on holiday					
llegar	to arrive					
llegar tarde	to be late					
llenar	to fill					
llevar	to take (a person), to wear					
llevar retraso	to be late					
mojarse	to get soaked					
molestar	to bother					
pasar	to spend (time), to happen					
quedar(se)	to stay					
rellenar un formulario	to fill in a form					
reservar	to book					
rodear	to surround					
sacar fotos	to take photos					
soler	to usually do something					
tardar	to take (time)					
tenderse al sol	to lie in the sun					
tomar	to take					
tomar el sol	to sunbathe					
tostarse	to sunbathe					
transportar	to transport					
veranear	to spend the summer					
viajar	to travel					
volar	to fly					

Abstractions

la afición	enthusiasm					
la alegría	happiness					
la ambición	ambition					
el cariño	affection					
el consejo	advice					
el cuidado	care					
el destino	destiny					

la duda	doubt
la escasez	scarcity
la esperanza	hope
el estado	state
la fama	fame
la forma	shape
la hospitalidad	hospitality
la importancia	importance
la infancia	childhood
la justicia	justice
la juventud	youth
la libertad	freedom
la manera	way
la memoria	memory
la meta	objective
el miedo	fear
la muerte	death
el orgullo	pride
la paciencia	patience
la pena	pity
la seguridad	security
el sentido	feeling
la siesta	nap
la suerte	luck
el tamaño	size
la verdad	truth

Expressions

¡adelante!	come in!
¡bienvenido!	welcome!
¡Dios mío!	gosh!
¡eso es!	that's it!
¡igualmente!	same to you!
¡Jesús!	bless you!
¡lástima!	what a shame!
¡madre mía!	gosh!
¡ni hablar!	out of the question!
¡oiga!	excuse me!
¡ojalá!	if only!
¡ojo!	careful!

MEG NEAB ULEAC SEG WJEC NICCEA

¡por Dios!	please do!
¡que aproveche!	enjoy your meal!
¡qué asco!	how disgusting!
¡qué bien!	how good!
¡qué horror!	how terrible!
¡qué lástima!	what a pity!
¡qué pena!	what a pity!
¡qué va!	no chance!
¡salud!	cheers!
¡socorro!	help!
¡suerte!	good luck!
¡tráigame!	bring me!
¡vale!	OK!
¿cómo es?	what is it like?
¿cómo estás	how are you?
¿cómo se dice ...?	how do you say ...?
¿cómo se escribe ...?	how do you spell ...?
¿de veras?	really?
¿qué hay?	what's new?
¿qué tal?	how are you?
¿se puede?	may I?
en absoluto	absolutely not!
adiós	goodbye
atentamente	Yours faithfully
buenas noches	good night
buenas tardes	good evening, good afternoon
buenos días	good day
claro	of course
conforme	agreed
de acuerdo	agreed
de nada	don't mention it
desde luego	of course
¡enhorabuena!	congratulations!
gracias	thank you
hasta la vista	see you soon
hasta luego	see you soon, later
hasta mañana	till tomorrow
hola	hello
lo siento	I'm sorry
me da igual	I don't mind

mucha suerte	good luck
muchas gracias	many thanks
mucho gusto	pleased to meet you
muy señor mío	Dear Sir (in a letter)
perdón	excuse me, sorry
perdona	excuse me
por ejemplo	for example
por eso	for that reason
por favor	please
por supuesto	of course
¡que aproveche!	enjoy your meal!
recuerdos	best wishes
saludos	greetings
vale la pena	it's worthwhile

Verbs

aconsejar	to advise
adivinar	to guess
admitir	to admit
advertir	to warn
agradecer	to thank
amenazar	to threaten
avisar	to warn
callarse	to be silent
convencer	to convince
decir	to say, to tell
declarar	to declare
disculparse	to say sorry
discutir	to discuss, to argue
felicitar	to congratulate
mencionar	to mention
mentir	to lie
sugerir	to suggest

Adjectives

agradecido	grateful
alegre	happy
animado	excited
atónito	astonished

cansado	tired
cariñoso	affectionate
constipado	having a cold
contento	happy
deprimido	depressed
encantado	delighted
enfadado	angry
enfermo	ill
favorito	favourite
feliz	happy
furioso	furious
harto	fed up
impaciente	impatient
inquieto	worried
ocupado	busy
orgulloso	proud
preocupado	worried
satisfecho	satisfied
triste	sad

Special occasions

Occasions

¡feliz santo!	Happy Saint's Day!
el Año Nuevo	New Year
la bandera	flag
la boda	wedding
el Corpus	Corpus Christi
la costumbre	custom
la cruz	cross
el cumpleaños	birthday
el día de fiesta	holiday
el día de mi santo	Saint's Day
el día de Navidad	Christmas Day
el día de Reyes	6th of January
el día festivo	non-working day
el día laboral	working day
Dios	God

el domingo de Resurrección	Easter Sunday
felices pascuas	Happy Easter/Christmas
felicidades	congratulations
feliz año nuevo	Happy New Year
feliz cumpleaños	Happy Birthday
feliz Navidad	Happy Christmas
la feria	holiday
la fiesta	holiday
los Juegos Olímpicos	Olympic Games
la luna de miel	honeymoon
la misa	mass
la mudanza	house move
la Navidad	Christmas
la Nochebuena	Christmas Eve
la Nochevieja	New Year's Eve
las Pascuas	Easter/Christmas
la procesión	procession
el sacerdote	priest
la Semana Santa	Holy Week
la verbena	fair
el Viernes Santo	Good Friday

Incidents

el accidente	accident
la acción	action
la ambulancia	ambulance
el asesinato	murder
el atraco	hold-up, mugging
la aventura	adventure
el aviso	warning
la ayuda	help
la bomba	bomb
la cárcel	gaol
el caso	case
el choque	collision
las circunstancias	circumstances
la contrabanda	smuggled goods
el crimen	crime
la Cruz Roja	Red Cross
el cuento	story

	MEG	NEAB	ULEAC	SEG	WJEC	NICCEA

el daño	damage
el delito	offence
el desastre	disaster
la descripción	description
la desgracia	misfortune
el engaño	deceipt
la escena	scene
el fuego	fire
el fusil	rifle
el golpe	blow
el grito	shout
el humo	smoke
el incendio	fire
la inundación	flood
la mentira	lie
el motivo	motive
la multa	fine
el peligro	danger
la pérdida	loss
la recompensa	reward
el rescate	rescue
el riesgo	risk
el robo	robbery
el salvavidas	life belt/jacket
la sangre	blood
el secuestro	kidnapping
la sorpresa	surprise
el suceso	event
el susto	fright
el testigo	witness
la tragedia	tragedy
la vida	life

The people

el asesino	murderer
el bombero	fireman
el/la cobarde	coward
el contrabandista	smuggler
el/la delincuente	delinquent
el drogadicto	drug addict

el/la guardia — policeman/woman
la Guardia Civil — police
el ladrón — thief
el/la policía — police officer
la policía — police
el ratero — pickpocket
la víctima — victim

Verbs

ahogarse — to drown
apagar — to put out (e.g. a fire)
aparecer — to appear
apresurarse — to hurry
asesinar — to murder
asustarse — to be frightened
atacar — to attack
atar — to tie
atracar — to rob, to mug
atreverse (a) — to dare (to)
atropellar — to run over
batir — to beat
batirse — to fight
ceda el paso — give way (when driving)
chocar (con) — to collide (with)
cometer — to commit
cruzar — to cross
denunciar — to report to the police
desaparecer — to disappear
describir — to describe
doblar la esquina — to turn the corner
engañar — to deceive
exigir — to demand
girar — to turn round
golpear — to hit
gritar — to shout
herirse — to get injured
identificarse — to identify oneself
imaginar — to imagine
obligar — to force
ocurrir — to happen

parar	to stop
pegar	to hit
proteger	to protect
quebrar	to break
realizar	to carry out
registrar	to search
rescatar	to rescue
robar	to steal
romper	to break
romperse	to break
salvar	to save
secuestrar	to kidnap
suceder	to happen

The world around us

Home town and local area

In the street

		MEG	NEAB	ULEAC	SEG	WJEC	NICCEA
la acera	pavement						
el banco	bench						
el buzón	post box						
la cabina telefónica	phone box						
la calle	street						
el carnet de identidad	ID card						
el cartel	poster						
la circulación	traffic						
el embotellamiento	traffic jam						
la esquina	corner						
el estanco	kiosk						
la fuente	fountain						
el letrero	sign						
la ley	law						
el monumento	monument						
la parada de autobuses	bus stop						
el paso de peatones	pedestrian crossing						
el peatón	pedestrian						
la persona mayor	adult						
la persona menor	young person						
prohibido el paso	no entry						
el ruido	noise						
el semáforo	traffic light						
el silencio	silence						
el surtidor	fountain						
el tráfico	traffic						
el transeúnte	passer-by						

The town

las afueras	outskirts						
el alcalde	mayor						
los alrededores	outskirts, surroundings						

	MEG	NEAB	ULEAC	SEG	WJEC	NICCEA
el aparcamiento	car park	•	•	•	•	•	•
el apartamento	flat	•	•	•	•	•	•
la arquitectura	architecture	•	•	•	•	•	•
la avenida	avenue	•	•	•	•	•	•
el ayuntamiento	building	•	•	•	•	•	•
el banco	bank	•	•	•	•	•	•
el bar	bar	•	•	•	•	•	•
el barrio	district	•	•	•	•	•	•
la bocacalle	side street	•	•	•	•	•	•
la calle	street	•	•	•	•	•	•
la capital	capital	•	•	•	•	•	•
el castillo	castle	•	•	•	•	•	•
el centro	centre	•	•	•	•	•	•
el centro comercial	shopping centre	•	•	•	•	•	•
la circulación	traffic	•	•	•	•	•	•
la ciudad	city	•	•	•	•	•	•
el ciudadano	citizen	•	•	•	•	•	•
el cruce	road junction	•	•	•	•	•	•
el edificio	building	•	•	•	•	•	•
la estatua	statue	•	•	•	•	•	•
la Guardia Civil	police	•	•	•	•	•	•
el parking	car park	•	•	•	•	•	•
el parque	park	•	•	•	•	•	•
el parque infantil	play ground	•	•	•	•	•	•
la parte	part	•	•	•	•	•	•
el piso	flat	•	•	•	•	•	•
el plano	town map	•	•	•	•	•	•
la plaza	square	•	•	•	•	•	•
la plaza mayor	main square	•	•	•	•	•	•
la población	population	•	•	•	•	•	•
el pueblo	small town, village	•	•	•	•	•	•
el puente	bridge	•	•	•	•	•	•
la situación	situation	•	•	•	•	•	•
la torre	tower	•	•	•	•	•	•
la urbanización	housing estate	•	•	•	•	•	•
la vecindad	vicinity	•	•	•	•	•	•
la vivienda	dwelling	•	•	•	•	•	•
la zona	area	•	•	•	•	•	•
la zona industrial	industrial area	•	•	•	•	•	•

The buildings

el albergue de juventud	youth hostel
el albergue juvenil	youth hostel
la biblioteca	library
la caja de ahorros	savings bank
la catedral	cathedral
el centro de deportes	sports centre
la comisaría	police station
correos	post office
la estación de autobuses	bus station
el hospital	hospital
la iglesia	church
el museo	museum
el museo de arte	art gallery
la oficina de correos	post office
la oficina de objetos perdidos	lost property office
la oficina de turismo	tourist office
el palacio	palace
la plaza de toros	bullring
el polideportivo	sports centre
el teatro	theatre

The shops

la agencia de viajes	travel agent's
la bodega	wine cellar
la carnicería	butcher's
la charcutería	pork butcher's
la churrería	fritter stall
la confitería	sweet shop
la droguería	drug store
la farmacia	chemist's
la frutería	fruit shop
la hamburguesería	hamburger outlet
la joyería	jeweller's
la lavandería	cleaner's
la librería	book shop
el mercado	market
el/la modista	dressmaker's
la panadería	baker's
la papelería	stationer's

MEG NEAB ULEAC SEG WJEC NICCEA

la pastelería	cake shop
la peluquería	hairdresser's
la perfumería	perfume shop
la pescadería	fish shop
la relojería	watch maker's
el tabacalero	tobacconist's
la tienda de comestibles	grocer's
la tienda de discos	record shop
la tienda de recuerdos	souvenir shop
la tienda de ultramarinos	grocer's
la verdulería	greengrocer's
la zapatería	shoe shop

Shopping

a mitad de precio	half price
la alimentación	food
los almacenes	stores
el artículo	article
el autoservicio	self-service
la bolsa	bag
el bolso	bag
el bote	tin
la caja	box
la caja	cash desk
la calidad	quality
el carro	supermarket trolley
la cesta	basket
el cesto	basket
el/la cliente	customer
la cola	queue
los comestibles	food
las compras	shopping
el coste	cost
el/la dependiente/a	shop assistant
el descuento	discount
el dinero	money
el escaparate	shop window
la falta	lack
el frasco	bottle
la ganga	bargain

los grandes almacenes	stores
el IVA	VAT
el kiosco	kiosk
la liquidación	sale
la lista	list
la muñeca	doll
el precio	price
el probador	fitting room
el producto	product
el puesto	stall
el quiosco	kiosk
la ranura	slot
las rebajas	reductions
el recibo	receipt
el recuerdo	souvenir
la sección de discos	record section
el segundo piso	second floor
el supermercado	supermarket
la talla	size
el tercer piso	third floor
la tienda	shop
el tipo	type
los ultramarinos	groceries
el valor	value
el/la vendedor/a	salesperson
la venta	sale

Shopping verbs

anunciar	to advertise
comprar	to buy
costar	to cost
desear	to wish
entregar	to deliver
enviar	to send
envolver	to wrap up
faltar	to lack
gastar	to spend (money)
introducir	to insert
ir de compras	to go shopping
mirar	to look at

mostrar	to show
pagar	to pay
pertenecer	to belong
pesar	to weigh
probarse	to try on
satisfacer	to satisfy
vender	to sell

The post office

el buzón	post box
la cabina telefónica	phone box
el código postal	post code
Correos	post office
la entrega	delivery
el paquete	parcel
el sello	stamp

The bank

el billete de banco	banknote
el cajero automático	cashpoint
el cambio	change
el céntimo	hundredth of a peseta
el cheque	cheque
el cheque de viajero	traveller's cheque
la comisión	commission
la cuenta de banco	bank account
el duro	five-peseta piece
la libra esterlina	pound sterling
la moneda	coin, currency
el penique	penny
la peseta (pta)	peseta
la sucursal	branch
el suelto	change
el talonario de cheques	cheque book
la tarjeta de crédito	credit card

Bank verbs

aceptar	to accept
aumentar	to increase

cambiar	to change
mandar	to send
obtener	to obtain
pedir prestado	to borrow
prestar	to lend
recibir	receive

The natural and made environment

Environment

el aire	air
la aldea	village
el aldeano	villager
el ambiente	atmosphere
el árbol	tree
el arroyo	stream
la bahía	bay
el bosque	wood
el camino	path
el/la campesino/a	peasant
el campo	countryside
la carretera	road
el cielo	sky
la colina	hill
el color	colour
la cosecha	harvest
el embalse	dam
la especie	type
la estrella	star
la flor silvestre	wild flower
la granja	farm
la isla	island
el lago	lake
la luna	moon
la marea	tide
la montaña	mountain
el mundo	world
la oscuridad	darkness

	MEG	NEAB	ULEAC	SEG	WJEC	NICCEA

el país	country
el paisaje	countryside
la península	peninsula
la piedra	stone
la pista	track
el prado	meadow
la provincia	province
la región	region
el río	river
la sierra	mountain range
el sonido	sound
la subida	climb
la tierra	earth, land
la valle	valley
la vertiente	slope

Animals

la abeja	bee
el animal	animal
la avispa	wasp
el burro	donkey
el caballito	pony
el caballo	horse
la cabra	goat
el cerdo	pig
el elefante	elephant
la gallina	hen
el insecto	insect
la mosca	fly
la oveja	sheep
el pájaro	bird
la paloma	dove
el pato	duck
el pavo	turkey
la rata	rat
la serpiente	snake
el tigre	tiger
el toro	bull
la vaca	cow

At the seaside

la arena	sand
la barca de pesca	fishing boat
el barco	boat
el chalet	villa
el colchón de aire	inflatable mattress
la costa	coast
el cubo	bucket
el mar	sea
la ola	wave
el parasol	parasol
la playa	beach
el puerto	port

The colours

amarillo	yellow
azul	blue
blanco	white
castaño	brown
el color naranja	orange
gris	grey
marrón	brown
moreno	dark
negro	black
rojo	red
rosado	pink
rubio	blond
verde	green

Adjectives

actual	present-day
apropiado	suitable
árido	arid
ecológico	ecological
eficaz	effective
físico	physical
internacional	international
militar	military
montañoso	mountainous

en paro	unemployed
plástico	plastic
tranquilo	quiet

Situations

¿por dónde se va a ...?	how do I get to ...?
al aire libre	in the open air
allá/allí	there
arriba	above, upstairs
la distancia	distance
en el suelo	on the floor
el fondo	bottom, far end
a la izquierda	on the left
el lado	side
el lugar	place
a orillas del mar	at the seaside
al revés	back to front
situado	situated
todo derecho	straight on
todo recto	straight on

Compass locations

el este	east
el noreste	northeast
el noroeste	northwest
el norte	north
el oeste	west
el sudeste	southeast
el sur	south
el suroeste	southwest

Places

la Costa Brava	Costa Brava
la Costa Cantábrica	Cantabrian Coast
la Costa del Sol	Costa del Sol
la Costa Verde	Green Coast
Londres	London

How much?

apenas	scarcely
aproximadamente	approximately
bastante	enough
completamente	completely
demasiado	too much
más	more
menos	less
mucho	a lot
poco	little
solamente	only
solo	alone
sólo	only
suficiente	sufficient
también	also

Where?

abajo	below, downstairs
adentro	inside
afuera	outside
ahí	there
allí	there
aquí	here
atrás	behind
dentro	inside
a la derecha	to the right
en alguna parte	somewhere
en casa	at home
en/por todas partes	everywhere
a la izquierda	to the left

How?

a pie	on foot
abierto	open
absolutamente	absolutely
afortunadamente	fortunately
andando	on foot
bien	well
casi	almost

de golpe	suddenly
de prisa	quickly
de veras	truly
desafortunadamente	unfortunately
desgraciadamente	unfortunately
despacio	slowly
exactamente	exactly
francamente	frankly
igualmente	equally
juntos	together
lentamente	slowly
mal	badly
muy bien	very well
naturalmente	of course
normalmente	normally
perfectamente	perfectly
por completo	completely
rápidamente	quickly
en realidad	really
sin duda	doubtless

When?

¿qué hora es?	what's the time?
a eso de	about
a menudo	often
a partir de	from
antes de	before
aún	still
al cabo de	at the end of
el comienzo	beginning
de costumbre	usually
de nuevo	again
de repente	suddenly
de vez en cuando	from time to time
dentro de poco	soon
después	after
el día	day
en punto	on the dot
entonces	then
la época	time

				MEG	NEAB	ULEAC	SEG	WJEC NICCEA

esta noche — tonight

la fecha — date

a fines de — at the end of

generalmente — usually

la hora — hour

la hora de comer — lunch time

el instante — instant

mientras tanto — meanwhile

muchas veces — often

otra vez — again

a partir de — from

pocas veces — rarely

por fin — finally

por lo general — in general

el principio — beginning

pronto — soon

de pronto — suddenly

raramente — rarely

un rato — a short while

en seguida — straight away

siempre — always

todavía — still

unas veces — sometimes

a veces — at times

la vez — occasion

ya — already

How long?

el año — year

el cuarto de hora — quarter of an hour

el fin de semana — weekend

la mañana — morning

media hora — half an hour

el mes — month

el minuto — minute

el momento — moment

la noche — night

ocho días — week

quince días — a fortnight

la semana — week

| el siglo | century |
| la tarde | evening |

Time expressions

actualmente	at present
ahora	now
ahora mismo	right now
algunas veces	sometimes
el año pasado	last year
anoche	last night
anteayer	the day before yesterday
ayer	yesterday
al día siguiente	on the following day
esta mañana	this morning
hace una hora	an hour ago
hoy	today
inmediatamente	straight away
las seis y pico	just after six o'clock
luego	then
la madrugada	very early in the morning
la medianoche	midnight
el mediodía	midday
pasado mañana	the day after tomorrow
por la mañana	in the morning
por la noche	at night
al principio	at the beginning
a principios	at the beginning of
recientemente	recently
las seis en punto	six o'clock exactly
temprano	early
todos los días	every day
últimamente	recently
la víspera	eve

The weather

bajo cero	below zero
la borrasca	storm
la brisa	breeze
la bruma	mist

el buen tiempo	good weather
el calor	heat
el chubasco	shower
el cielo	sky
el clima	climate
la escarcha	frost
la estación del año	season
la gota	drop
el grado	degree
hace buen tiempo	the weather is nice
hace fresco	the weather is cool
hace mal tiempo	the weather is bad
hace sol	the weather is sunny
hace viento	the weather is windy
hacer calor	to be hot
hacer frío	to be cold
el hielo	ice
la humedad	humidity
la lluvia	rain
el mal tiempo	bad weather
la neblina	mist
la niebla	fog
la nieve	snow
la nube	cloud
la nubosidad	cloudiness
el pronóstico del tiempo	weather forecast
el relámpago	lightning
el sol	sun
la temperatura	temperature
la tempestad	storm
el tiempo	weather
la tormenta	storm
el trueno	thunder
el viento	wind

Weather adjectives

anublado	cloudy
caluroso	hot
cubierto	cloudy
despejado	clear

fresco	cool, fresh
frío	cold
húmedo	humid
nublado	cloudy
oscuro	dark
soleado	sunny
templado	mild

Weather verbs

brillar	to shine
cosechar	to harvest
guardar	to keep
llover	to rain
nevar	to snow
soplar	to blow
tronar	to thunder

Shapes and sizes

alto	tall
ambos	both
amplio	wide
ancho	wide
bastante	enough
cada	each
corto	short
cuadrado	square
delgado	thin
doble	double
enorme	enormous
estrecho	narrow
flaco	thin
gordo	fat
grande	big
grueso	fat
inmenso	immense
insuficiente	insufficient
largo	long
máximo	maximum
mayor	bigger

				MEG		
			NEAB			
			ULEAC			
		SEG				
		WJEC				
		NICCEA				

mediano	middling
medio	average, half
menor	smaller
mínimo	minimum
normal	normal
pequeño	small
profundo	deep
tanto	so much, so many
todo	all
varios	several

People and things

Positive adjectives

activo	active
agradable	pleasant
amable	pleasant
ambicioso	ambitious
aplicado	hard-working
atrevido	daring
capaz	capable
célebre	famous
chulo	amusing, attractive
cortés	polite
curioso	curious
de buen humor	good-humoured
de buena salud	healthy
deportivo	sporting (i.e. likes sport)
directo	direct
dispuesto	ready
divertido	amusing
elegante	elegant
emocionante	exciting
encantador	delightful
enérgico	energetic
espléndido	splendid
Estimado	Dear (in letters)
estupendo	marvellous

excelente	excellent
famoso	famous
fantástico	fantastic
fenomenal	marvellous
formal	well-behaved
fuerte	strong
generoso	generous
gracioso	funny
guapo	handsome, pretty
histórico	historic
honesto	honest
honrado	honorable
inocente	innocent
inteligente	intelligent
interesante	interesting
justo	just, fair, right
limpio	clean
lindo	pretty
listo	ready, clever
maravilloso	marvellous
mejor	better
nuevo	new
paciente	patient
perfecto	perfect
positivo	positive
práctico	practical
precioso	lovely
sano	healthy
santo	holy
seguro	safe
sensible	sensitive
serio	serious, reliable
simpático	nice
sobresaliente	outstanding
trabajador	hardworking
útil	useful
valiente	brave
verdadero	true
vivo	alive

Negative adjectives

agresivo	aggressive
antipático	unpleasant
borracho	drunk
callado	quiet
celoso	suspicious, jealous
cruel	cruel
culpable	guilty
de mal humor	bad-humoured
débil	weak
desafortunado	unfortunate
desagradable	unpleasant
descortés	rude
difícil	difficult
egoísta	selfish
equivocado	mistaken
estúpido	stupid
falso	false
fatal	very bad
feo	ugly
goloso	greedy
grave	serious
hablador	talkative
horrible	horrible
imposible	impossible
insoportable	unbearable
inútil	useless
loco	mad
mal educado	rude
malo	bad
mareado	sea-sick, dizzy
mentiroso	lying
nervioso	nervous
peor	worse
perezoso	lazy
regular	so so
roto	broken
ruidoso	noisy
salvaje	wild
sospechoso	suspicious

MEG NEAB ULEAC SEG WJEC NICCEA

sucio	dirty
terrible	terrible
tonto	silly
torpe	clumsy
travieso	naughty
vacío	empty

Physical adjectives

agudo	sharp
anticuado	old
automático	automatic
bello	beautiful
breve	brief
bueno	good
caliente	warm, hot
céntrico	central
cercano	nearby
cerrado	closed
cierto	certain, true
comercial	commercial
con retraso	late
concurrido	crowded
dañoso	harmful
de moda	in fashion
delantero	front
diferente	different
distinto	different
duro	hard
eléctrico	electric
electrónico	electronic
especial	special
espeso	thick
exterior	exterior
extraño	strange
extraordinario	extraordinary
ferroviario	rail
flojo	weak
futuro	future
hermoso	beautiful
industrial	industrial

intacto	intact
lejano	distant
lento	slow
ligero	light
liso	smooth
lleno	full
mojado	soaked, wet
nacido	born
natural	natural
peligroso	dangerous
pesado	heavy
quieto	still
rápido	fast
raro	strange
real	royal
reciente	recent
redondo	round
seco	dry
sencillo	single (ticket)
sentado	sitting
siguiente	following
suave	soft
tibio	lukewarm
tímido	shy
típico	typical
trasero	rear
último	last
único	only
urgente	urgent

The world of work

Job applications

Work

		MEG	NEAB	ULEAC	SEG	WJEC	NICCEA
el acuerdo	agreement						
la ambición	ambition						
el anuncio	advertisement						
la carrera	race						
el comercio	trade						
la compañía	company						
la computadora	computer						
el contrato	contract						
el despacho	office						
el ejército	army						
el empleo	job						
la empresa	firm						
la entrevista	interview						
el escritorio	desk, office						
la fábrica	factory						
la finca	farm						
la formación	training						
el formulario	form						
la fotocopia	photocopy						
la ganancia	profit						
la hoja de solicitud	job application form						
el impuesto	tax						
la industria	industry						
la máquina	machine						
la máquina de escribir	typewriter						
los negocios	business						
la oferta	offer						
la oficina	office						
la profesión	profession						
el proyecto	plan						
la reunión	meeting						
el salario	salary						
el sindicato	trades union						

el sueldo	pay
el taller	workshop
la taquigrafía	shorthand
el trabajo	work
el turismo	tourism
la universidad	university

The people

el amo	boss
el/la aprendiz/a	apprentice
el/la colega	colleague
el/la empleado/a	employee
el empresario	businessman
el/la encargado/a	employee in charge
el/la gerente	manager
el/la jefe/a	boss
el patrón	boss
el/la responsable	person in charge
el sindicalista	trades union member

Verbs

acostumbrarse	to get used to
cubrir	to cover
cuidar	to take care of
cultivar	to grow
diseñar	to design
disfrutar	to enjoy
distinguir	to distinguish
emplear	to employ
escribir	to write
escribir a máquina	to type
estar de pie	to be standing
estar en paro	to be unemployed
estar sentado	to be sitting
ganarse la vida	to earn your living
haber	to have
hablar	to speak, to talk
hacer	to do, to make
hacer falta	to need

hacer una encuesta	to conduct a survey
hacerse	to become
interpretar	to play the part
jubilarse	to retire
pagar	to pay
recomendar	to recommend
recompensar	to reward
remitir adjunto	to enclose
reunirse	to meet together
ser	to be
tener	to have
trabajar	to work
trabajar de canguro	to babysit

Jobs

el abogado	lawyer
el actor	actor
la actriz	actress
el aduanero	customs officer
el/la agente	agent
el ama de casa (f)	housewife
el arquitecto	architect
el/la artista	artist
el/la autor/a	author
la azafata	air hostess
el basurero	rubbish collector
el bombero	fireman
el/la camarero/a	waiter/waitress
el camionero	lorry driver
el/la cantante	singer
el carnicero	butcher
el carpintero	carpenter
el cartero	postman
el chófer	driver
el científico	scientist
el/la cocinero/a	cook
el/la comerciante	shopkeeper
el cómico	comedian
el/la conductor/a	driver

	MEG	MEG	MEG	NEAB	ULEAC	SEG	SEG	WJEC	NICCEA

la criada — maid
el cura — priest
el dentista — dentist
el/la dependiente/a — shop assistant
el doctor — doctor
el/la electricista — electrician
el/la enfermero/a — nurse
el/la escritor/a — writer
el/la espía — spy
el/la farmacéutico/a — chemist
el/la florista — florist
el fontanero — plumber
el fotógrafo — photographer
el frutero — fruitseller
el funcionario — civil servant
el/la garajista — garage attendant
el granjero — farmer
el/la guardia — policeman/woman
el guardián — warden
el/la guía — guide
el hombre de negocios — businessman
el ingeniero — engineer
el inspector — inspector
el jardinero — gardener
el juez — judge
el lechero — milkman
el/la maestro/a — teacher (primary school)
el marinero — sailor
el mecánico — mechanic
la mecanógrafa — typist
el minero — miner
la mujer de negocios — businesswoman
el negociante — trader
el obrero — worker
el panadero — baker
el/la peluquero/a — hairdresser
el/la periodista — journalist
el pescador — fisherman
el piloto — pilot
el pintor — painter

el profesor	teacher (secondary)
el químico	chemist
el/la recepcionista	receptionist
el/la representante	representative
el sastre	tailor
el/la secretario/a	secretary
el soldado	soldier
el técnico	technician
el tendero	shopkeeper

Communication

The telephone

la central telefónica	telephone exchange
el cobro revertido	reverse-charge
la conferencia	long-distance call
el contestador automático	answering machine
la guía telefónica	telephone book
la llamada	call
el número de teléfono	phone number
el prefijo	code
el recado	message
el teléfono	telephone

Telephone verbs

contestar	to answer
descolgar	to pick up the phone
equivocarse	to make a mistake
estar equivocado	to be mistaken
llamar	to call
llamar por teléfono	to phone
marcar	to dial
oír	to hear
telefonear	to phone

GCSE Spanish Vocabulary Book

Telephone expressions

¡al aparato!	speaking!
¡diga!	hello!
¡dígame!	hello!
está comunicando	engaged
no cuelgue Vd.	hold the line

Useful IT vocabulary

reserva; de seguridad; salvaguardar	back-up
lenguaje BASIC	BASIC
negrita	bold
inicialización; inicializar; cebar	boot
exploración; examen (de la información)	browsing
error; gazapo; basura	bug
Enseñanza Asistida por Ordenador (EAO)	Computer-Assisted Learning
técnico informático	computer professional
cursor	cursor
desplazar; trasladar (la información en la pantalla)	cut and paste
dato; referencia	datum
base de datos	database
sistema de gestión de base de datos	database management system
borrar; suprimir	delete
autoedición (producción autónoma de publicaciones de calidad)	desktop publishing
directorio; repertorio	directory
sistema operativo en disco (DOS)	disc operating system (DOS)
unidad de disco	disc-drive
visualizar; presentar	display
telecarga de programas	downloading of programs
transcribir (imprimir una presentación de pantalla)	dump (print out a screen)
revisar; corregir; modificar; preparar (el texto)	edit
revisión; corrección; edición	editing
programas de aplicación didácticos (equipo lógico)	educational software
correo electrónico	electronic mail

MEG MEG MEG NEAB ULEAC SEG WJEC NICCEA

84

facsímil (fax)	facsimile (fax)
campo; sección (en una base de datos)	field (on database)
ficha; fichero; archivo	file
disquete; disco flexible	floppy disc
formatear (un disquete virgen o una visualización)	format (a blank disc or display)
tecla de función	function key
copia integral (presentación impresa); copia impresora	hard copy (a print-out)
disco duro; disco rígido	hard disc
hardware; aparatos integrantes	hardware
realce; realzar	highlighting
informática; tecnología de la información	information technology
input; entrada	input
interactivo	interactive
tecla	key
teclado	keyboard
palabra clave; palabra reservada	keyword
cargar un programa	load a program
carga	loading
menú	menu
unir; fusionar	merge
microprocesador; microplaqueta	microchip
microordenador; microcomputadora	microcomputer
módem	modem
monitor; pantalla	monitor
ratón	mouse
calidad correspondencia; impresión de alta calidad	Near Letter Quality (NLQ)
red informática	network
desconectado; fuera de línea; autónomo	off-line
ofimática	office technology
conectado; en línea	on-line
salida	output
paquete; juego de programas	package
contraseña	password
periférico	peripheral
gráfico de sectores	pie chart
impresora	printer
programa	program

señal; indicación visible (demanda de respuesta)	prompt (input request)
memoria de acceso aleatorio (RAM); memoria de lectura-escritura	Random Access Memory (RAM)
memoria de lectura solamente (ROM); memoria permanente	Read Only Memory (ROM)
registro (en una base de datos)	record (in a database)
archivar; almacenar	save
pantalla	screen
visualización en pantalla	screen display
corrimiento; movimiento de avance/ retroceso de imagen en la pantalla	scrolling
programa; software	software
hoja electrónica	spreadsheet
pila	stack (Apple Hypercard)
cadena de caracteres	string (unit of characters/numbers)
telecomunicaciones	telecommunications
videotexto	teletext
terminal	terminal
programa de servicio; utilidad	utility (program to support software)
información visualizada videotex/teletex	viewdata
sintetizador de voz	voice synthesiser
tratamiento de textos	word-processing
procesador de textos	word-processor
(lo que usted ve es lo que se imprimirá) = salida visualizada definitiva (SVD)	WYSIWYG (what you see is what you get)

The international world

Tourism at home and abroad

Transport

Spanish	English	MEG	NEAB	ULEAC	SEG	WJEC	NICCEA
la aduana	customs						
el aeropuerto	airport						
la agencia de viajes	travel agent's						
el asiento	seat						
el aterrizaje	landing						
la autopista	motorway						
el autostop	hitchhiking						
la autovía	main road						
el billete	ticket						
el billete de ida	single ticket						
el billete de ida y vuelta	return ticket						
la bolsa	bag						
el bonobús	bus pass						
el canal	canal						
la carretera	road						
el control de pasaportes	passport check						
el cruce	road junction						
la curva peligrosa	dangerous bend						
la demora	delay						
con destino a	heading for						
el equipaje	luggage						
la estación de autobuses	bus station						
la estación de servicio	service station						
el extranjero	abroad						
el folleto	brochure						
la frontera	border						
el gasoil	diesel oil						
el/la guía	guide						
la guía	guide-book						
el horario	timetable						
la huelga	strike						
la línea aérea	airline						
la llegada	arrival						

la maleta	suitcase
el metro	underground train
las obras	roadworks
el peaje	motorway toll
la prisa	speed
la reserva	reservation
el retraso	delay
el terminal	terminal
el transporte	transport
las vacaciones	holidays
el viaje	journey
el/la viajero/a	traveller
el vuelo	flight
la vuelta	return

The people

el aduanero	customs officer
el/la autostopista	hitchhiker
la azafata	air hostess
el cobrador	ticket-collector
el/la fumador/a	smoker
el/la garajista	garage attendant
el/la habitante	inhabitant
la motocicleta	motorcyclist
el/la pasajero/a	passenger
el revisor	ticket inspector

Vehicles

el autobús	bus
el autocar	coach
el avión	plane
el camión	lorry
el ferry	ferry
el helicóptero	helicopter
la moto	motorcycle
el taxi	taxi
el tranvía	tram

By car

el aceite	oil
el asiento	seat
el auto	car
el/la automovilista	driver
la avería	breakdown
la batería	battery
el carnet de conducir	driving licence
el cinturón de seguridad	safety belt
el coche	car
el depósito	fuel tank
el desvío	detour
el embotellamiento	traffic jam
el faro	headlight
los frenos	brakes
la gasolina	petrol
la gasolinera	filling station
la marca	make
el mecánico	mechanic
el modelo	model
el motor	engine
el neumático	tyre
el parabrisas	windscreen
el permiso de conducir	driving licence
el pinchazo	puncture
la portezuela	door (of vehicle)
la reparación	repair
la rueda	wheel
sin plomo	lead-free
el súper	high-grade petrol
el tornillo	screw
el vehículo	vehicle
la velocidad	speed
la ventanilla	window (of vehicle)
el volante	steering wheel
la zona azul	blue zone (parking)

By train

el andén	platform
el asiento	seat
el billete sencillo	single ticket
el coche cama	sleeping car
el coche restaurante	dining car
la consigna	left-luggage
la correspondencia	rail connection
el departamento	compartment
el despacho de billetes	ticket office
la estación	station
la estación del ferrocarril	railway station
el ferrocarril	railway
de largo recorrido	long distance
el mozo	porter
la primera clase	first class
procedente de	coming from
la red	network
RENFE	Spanish Railways
la sala de espera	waiting room
la segunda clase	second class
el suplemento	supplement
Talgo	luxury train
la taquilla	ticket office
transbordar	to change trains
el transbordo	connection
el tren	train
el tren expreso	express train
la vía	track

Countries

Alemania	Germany
América del Sur	South America
Argentina	Argentina
Australia	Australia
Austria	Austria
Bélgica	Belgium
Chile	Chile
EE.UU	USA

Escocia	Scotland
España	Spain
Estados Unidos	U.S.A.
Europa	Europe
Francia	France
Gales	Wales
Gran Bretaña	Great Britain
Grecia	Greece
Holanda	Holland
Inglaterra	England
Irlanda	Ireland
Irlanda del Norte	Northern Ireland
Italia	Italy
Méjico/México	Mexico
el País de Gales	Wales
Perú	Peru
Portugal	Portugal
el Reino Unido	United Kingdom
Rusia	Russia
Suecia	Sweden
Suiza	Switzerland
Venezuela	Venezuela

Nationalities

alemán (alemana f)	German
americano	American
argentino	Argentinian
austríaco	Austrian
belga	Belgium
británico	British
chileno	Chilean
escocés (escocesa f)	Scottish
español	Spanish
europeo	European
extranjero	foreigner
francés (francesa f)	French
galés (galesa f)	Welsh
griego	Greek
holandés	Dutch

inglés (inglesa f)	English
irlandés (irlandesa f)	Irish
italiano	Italian
mejicano/mexicano	Mexican
norteamericano	American
peruano	Peruvian
portugués (portuguesa f)	Portuguese
ruso	Russian
sudamericano	South American
sueco	Swedish
suizo	Swiss
venezolano	Venezuelan

Life in other countries and communities

Rivers

el Duero	Duero River
el Ebro	Ebro River
el Guadalquivir	Guadalquivir River
el Manzanares	Manzanares River
el Tajo	Tagus River

Regions

Andalucía	Andalusia
Asturias	Asturias
Castilla	Castille
Cataluña	Catalonia
Euskadi	Basque Country
Extremadura	Extremadura
Galicia	Galicia
Mancha	Mancha Region
el País Vasco	Basque Country
Vizcaya	Biscay province

People

| andaluz | Andalusian |
| asturiano | from Asturias |

	cantábrico	Cantabrian
castellano	native of Castille
catalán (catalana f)	Catalan
el forastero	stranger
el gallego	native of Galicia
el judío	Jew
vasco	Basque

Mountains

los Alpes	the Alp
la Sierra de Guadarrama	Guadarrama mountains
los Pirineos	the Pyrenees
la Sierra Nevada	Sierra Nevada mountains

Seas

| el Atlántico | Atlantic |
| el Mediterráneo | Mediterranean Sea |

World events and issues

Problems

la actitud	attitude
la agricultura	agriculture
la basura	rubbish
la causa	cause
la comparación	comparison
la conclusión	conclusion
la contaminación	pollution
el desempleo	unemployment
la diferencia	difference
la discusión	argument
en mi opinión	in my opinion
la encuesta	survey
la ética	ethics
la explicación	explanation
la guerra (mundial)	(world) war
el hambre (f)	hunger, famine

el hecho	fact	
la idea	idea	
el inconveniente	disadvantage	
la inmigración	immigration	
la lucha	struggle	
la manifestación	demonstration	
la mayoría	majority	
la medida	measure	
el medio ambiente	environment	
el Mercado Común	Common Market	
el nivel	level	
la ocasión	opportunity	
la opinión	opinion	
el partido	party (political)	
la paz	peace	
la política	politics	
el problema	problem	
la razón	reason	
la reacción	reaction	
la religión	religion	
la seguridad social	social security	
el servicio militar	military service	
el sueño	dream	
la tendencia	tendency	
la tradición	tradition	
UE (Unión Europea)	European Community	
la ventaja	advantage	

People

el gobierno	government	
la marina	navy	
la muchedumbre	crowd	
la ONU	UNO	
el/la optimista	optimist	
el/la pesimista	pessimist	
el político	politician	
la princesa	princess	
el príncipe	prince	
el/la protestante	Protestant	

la reina	queen
el rey	king
la sociedad	society
el/la terrorista	terrorist

Verbs

conservar	to conserve
construir	to build
contaminar	to pollute
contener	to contain
creer	to believe
decidir	to decide
depender de	to depend on
destruir	to destroy
dudar	to hesitate
eliminar	to eliminate
estar a favor de	to be in favour of
estar al día	to be up to date
estar de acuerdo	to agree
estar en contra de	to be against
existir	to exist
hacer la mili	to do military service
hay	there is, there are
hay que	it is necessary
justificar tu opinión	to justify your opinion
juzgar	to judge
manifestar	to demonstrate
mejorarse	to improve
opinar	to think that
pensar	to think
preguntarse	to wonder
saber	to know
suponer	to suppose
tender	to tend
tratar de	to try to